CHRISTMAS IS COMING

Christmas is Coming

An Erotic Poetry Collection

Micky Omega

TABLE OF CONTENTS

Baking Cookies

I am on my third day of baking the week
of Christmas, filling tins and tupperware
with sweets I can never hope to finish
and so will foist on my family and coworkers.

My lover slips into the kitchen, hair mussed
from sleep on this precious day of rest.
When his cup of coffee warms in the microwave,
he presses his chest to my back.

The flour on my apron imprints on his wrist
much the same way the wet of his precum
stains the hairs of my bare ass as he grinds
against me. *I like your uniform.*

His hot tub breath warms my winter ears.
There's a chill to the house, nude in an apron,
made colder in contrast to his inferno.
I arch back against him as if else I'll get frostbite.

The microwave beeps intermittently as the coffee
returns to its lukewarm state in its prison,
longing for those same lips that press needy
against my shivering, bruising neck.

It becomes the R&B soundtrack to our mid-afternoon
morning fuck. It mixes with the squelch of vegetable
oil around his cock as he fills me. My moans
harmonize with his own. Christmas is coming.

Micky Omega

I've dreamt of such filthy romantic domesticity
since I first lost my virginity. This is what it is
to be so loved, not an inch in the house is free
of traces from our mixing and melding and baking.

When his cum dribbles as icing out my hole
and down my thigh, he'll restart the microwave.
He'll make us both a gourmet lunch as he chats
about his nonsense dreams. *I was a snow prince.*

Once upon a time, his tongue couldn't stand
sweets. Now he is one of those Buckingham soldiers,
famously unmovable, resolute, sticking out a pinky
because my treats are fancy delicacies.

After lunch, we stand over the stand mixer,
kissing greedy like our stomachs are empty,
cocks rubbing against each other. Our loads
spill into the batter for a batch meant only for us.

I always underestimate the amount of butter I'll need.
He grabs his keys before I can find my pants,
slaps my ass, and kisses my forehead.
Be back soon, cute stuff.

He returns with a bottle of wine and another of mead.
There's butter, too, and a frozen pizza for tonight.
It's hard not to cry in his arms. It's harder not to cum.
This is the sexiest thing. This is love.

Santa's Lap

If there's one thing that universal lie
parents slap out here in America got right,
it's that the way to get gifts out of a man
is to sit right on his knee, on his lap,
and bounce.

*I promise I've been a good boy. Bad boys
don't feel like velvet on the inside like I do.
They don't worship at the altar of a good man
like I do. Treat me right, Santa. I promise
I've been a good boy.*

Mistletoe

You kiss under the mistletoe, so on the first
day of Christmas, I gift him a winter garden
printed on boxer briefs. As he pulls them up,
I go down. I am a succubus in the morning.
My lips press into his thighs, over the rolling
hills of his ass, singing *The Sound of Music*
against the fabric. I kiss his basket of gifts,
his wrapped Yule log, and the hidden foliage
of his untrimmed hedges. He grabs me
by the face. *You kiss under the mistletoe*,
he reminds me. Quick as they dressed him,
the underwear is gone. My tongue bathes
his skin. His fingers run through my hair.
His sighs speak of more holy music than any
Christmas Carol could dare to touch.
The briefs join his holiday pajama set, and
I send my love to sleep each night
with kisses on the green.

Ugly Sweater

It's such a crime against my eyes, he says,
*I want to rip it off of you. I want the seams
to tear like Christmas wrapping paper.
I want the threads to unravel like my mind
when you sit next to me and make your
stupid little jokes with your stupid little face
being too cute for me to handle. I want
you to stand shirtless with that pink paint
you get when I tease you. I bet your nipples
are the only hairy part of your chest. I bet
they get hard at the slightest breeze. I bet
you cover them with your hands like you know
how beautiful they are and you're trying to protect
the rest of us from having to see something so
grand and then move on with our lives.
It's such an ugly sweater.*

He takes it off me at two in the morning
barely past the door to my apartment.

St. Gabriel

There's an angel sat atop the tree
with Christmas shoved up his ass
and a heavenly, unbothered grin
on his face, watching us roll
around in front of the fireplace.

We are being held in the gaze
of Heaven, serene and blessing,
my love, encouraging our white Christmas
like God himself is saying,
Y'all fuck like angels.

I can feel the Holy Spirit move through me
the exact same way your cum does
when you cry out and thrust with your
eyes clenched, as if you balls
are where Heaven is stored.

St. Gabriel has come to deliver a message
from up on high that there has never
been a thing so holy as the way
our lips press into each other
when we are done making love.

Christmas Card

On the first day of Christmas,
my true love gave to me: my cock
caged up in chastity.

He took that tiny key, small as a crumb,
and stole it away for the holiday season
like a grinning Grinch.

Taking and swallowing his egg nog
is the closest I get to cumming
for that first week of December.

My balls become Christmas ornaments,
blue, sparkling, and fragile, hanging from
a tree disallowed from growth.

I drape my legs as garland on his shoulders
as my true love gives me my second gift:
my first fountain-orgasm from only his cock.

I've never been so horny in my life. I suck
him on the way to the airport. I steal him
into the bathroom. I cling to his arms.

At his parents' house, he stuffs my mouth
with his Christmas stocking so my moans
won't wake the house on Christmas Eve.

The night we return to our house, the day
after Christmas, when we are the only ones
in the world, he hands me an envelope.

Micky Omega

A calligrapher's landscape love letter paints
the cardstock. My eyes water. It's cold out,
so it starts to snow in our bedroom.

A little baggy sits on the back of the card.
The key to the cage sits insides with a small
note: *For my good boy.*

On the last day of Christmas, my true love
gave to me: a freed cock oiled up and kissed
for hours as if to make up for its time in prison.

I cum once all over his face. He Santa laughs
and kissed me. We swap my semen, and then
he's back to worshiping my sex.

I lose count of how many times he brings me
to the edge, past the brink. I shiver after
the blizzard ends and his love keeps coming.

The next morning, he wakes me with his cock
sliding in and out of my hole. His stomach barely
touches me, and I spurt. I beg. I moan.

When he collapses on top of me, he whispers,
Let me know if you want to be locked again.
I'll gladly make you mine and mine alone.

Rudolph

had a shiny nose?
More like a shiny head!

You can't stop your eyes
from rolling back.

This is your fault for letting me
give your dick nicknames.

For Christmas, it is Rudolph,
with its glistening ruby tip.

Like Rudy, it, too will go down
in history, in folk song, in myth.

History can be your nickname
for my hole, if you want.

Rudolph can go *in* and then *out*
instead of *down.*

When I walk out of the shower,
it's a steamy, foggy Christmas Eve.

History needs Rudolph
to show me the way.

Ralphie

You're gonna shoot your eye out!
See, but here's the thing, the risk
is worth it. If I'm going to go blind
because you fired ammo out your
balls and all over my face, then dammit,
I was born to be blind. I'll miss your face,
but when I'm out of the hospital, you know
the first thing I'm going to do is get down
on my knees and demand you shoot
out the other eye, too. My Christmas wish
is to be tongue-stuck to your pole,
to decode the quakes of your thighs,
to drip with your semen when we order
Chinese food and laugh, baby,
laugh away the night.

Eggnog

If you want me to drink
something bitter, white,
and frothing, then baby
boy, push me down
to my knees and let me
take it right from the tap,
because there's no way
on God's green Earth
I'm drinking any other
sort of eggnog.

Glass of Milk

All the TikTok influencers and Twitter pornstars
hock this pill they claim increases the production
of seminal fluid. *Order with my code to get 2%
off on your gallons of milk!* Let's run an experiment,
my love, the day of Christmas Eve. You'll take
these cum-gushers and I'll tie you all-fours on the
bed. We can listen to Christmas music or watch
holiday films or, even better, Christmas porn
where twinks salivate over each other in Santa hats
and Santa-bears pull naughty boys over their knees.
I'll grab a glass from the kitchen cabinet to take
every load you're going to leak. I'll rub your back
and kiss your feet and gently pulse a vibrator
in your hairy, pulsing hole. My slick fingers will draw
forth moans from your nipples and shaft. I will kiss
your overtime-working sweatshop sack and call you
a good boy, a good cow, my handsome, sexy man
letting me bathe you in unending pleasure. Soon,
we will have a glass of warm milk for Santa
to take in the night when you slumber in my arms.

Elves, Shelves, Twinks, Drinks

You've heard of *Elf on the Shelf?*
Now get ready for a bear in your derriere.

Now get ready for a cock in a sock.
Now get ready for a twunk on your junk.

Now get ready for a lip on your nip.
Now get ready for an otter to cover in slobber.

Now get ready for a cub to rub.
Now get ready for a chub in need of a sub.

Now get ready for a pup sat ass-up.
Now get ready for a sir to make you sore.

Now get ready to not stop and think
because you need to top a twink.

Now get ready to fast offer up that ass.
Now get ready for my cum in your bum.

The Christmas party is an orgy for any elf
who wants to find love outside himself.

Micky Omega

Fruitcake

People claim they would rather die
than eat a fruitcake. Sounds dramatic.

See, I would die to eat a fruitcake.
Smother me in your loaves, hot stuff.

Place all that batter right on my face
and let me feast all night long.

There's something about feeling warmth
from cheeks pressed against your cheeks.

People who don't eat ass but are curious
often ask we connoisseurs what it tastes like.

It tastes like ambrosia, my friends, like a cake
baked with the apples of immortality.

It tastes like falling out of your own head
and into a place where nothing bad can happen.

It tastes like the first time you sang in the shower
and passingly thought that maybe you're a singer.

It tastes like telling a joke muffled in his hole and
repeating it when he gets off, both of you laughing.

It tastes like melting into your sheets and sinking
deep into the baked crust of the Earth.

It tastes like wading into the raging ocean
and floating like driftwood on the waves.

Christmas is Coming

It tastes like making a lame joke about fruitcake
and having your fruity lover serve you his cake.

To eat ass is to trust someone with your life.
I will request fruitcake as my last supper.

Micky Omega

Frosty the Sexdoll

After the movie marathon, I jokingly
placed a tophat on my big-dicked
sex doll I pretend is my boyfriend
when I'm going through a dry spell.

A cold wind blew through the apartment
and swirled around his silicone skin
until his blue eyes began to blink
and his skin grew warm to the touch.

We screamed back and forth
for a solid two minutes thirty seconds –
we had to make sure it was long enough
to be a song in the inevitable film.

I named him Frosty because my mind broke
when he asked what his name was.
Apparently he asked so we could both know
what to moan out when he'd get to fucking me.

Frosty the Sexdoll was a very jolly soul.
He didn't desire adventures out in the sun,
though we took those anyway. He wanted
kisses and sex and romance.

His dildo cock pounded at my hole and mouth.
He loved to orgasm within me, though
he was jealous he couldn't shower me
in cum the same way I could him.

Christmas is Coming

His favorite movies were the John Wick flicks
which he claimed were romantic Christmas movies.
You can just tell he really loved her, he said
with a wistfulness most men can only dream of.

We dance under the glittering lights of the tree.
Christmas songs play on the TV while a fireplace
loops through the same two minutes of swaying flames.
I end up on my knees in the purple night.

I am no longer lonely in the holiday season.
I have fallen in love with my dildo and pocket pussy.
Frosty holds me in the mornings, and kisses
me while we whisper deep in my bed.

My sex doll has met my friends and family.
He's a published poet and popular poster
of his polished north pole. Next Christmas,
I think he and I will marry in the snow.

I suppose the lesson is: place hats on everything.
Magic is a curious beast that might strike
at any time. Now even when he takes the tophat off,
my Frosty love remains his jolly self.

Micky Omega

Candy Cane I

The shepherd's hook is there
not to hang from a tree, like
people commonly think –
It's candy, not an ornament.
But it's the perfect bend
to wrap a finger around
when you push the swirling mint
in and out of my wet and pulsing
hole, teasing it with your cool
breath, promising if I'm a good
boy, you'll replace the candy
with your own cane in the sticky sweet.

Caroler

There's this twink who goes around
caroling all by himself every year.
When I asked why he doesn't get the other
kids at his college to join him wandering
through the neighborhood, he reveals
he's in his thirties with a cushy tech job
which I suppose makes sense for why he lives
in such an expensive neighborhood by himself.

My fiance and I greet him at the stoop
with figgy pudding and invite him in
so he might warm his pink cheeks
from the gentle freeze on the breeze.
If you ever want to take someone to France,
the first thing to do is compliment their singing,
mention how it's nearly as pretty as their face,
their eyes, the kindness in their voice.

He's singing Carol of the Bells as my man
presses his face in and out of my ass.
He's singing Jingle Bells as mine dangle
over his lips and my fiance loosens his hole.
He's singing silent night as I hold him and that
perfect cock plunges in and out of his hole.
He can't sing when his tongue is busy
wrapped around my throat plunging north pole.

Micky Omega

The caroling twink rolls back around
three days later with a deeper pink on his cheeks.
When the door opens, he starts to carol
even though Christmas is over. He says
the Eiffel Tower, the Seine, and the streets of Paris
are too irresistible to visit only once, especially
when visiting is such an easy time. He comes
inside and we cum inside him.

The Drummer Boy

gives out his marching orders
via smacks on the bongos
at his waist. The sound
is different when they're covered
in the red fabric of briefs and when
they're bare except for hair.
The nude drums grow red
as the seasonal underwear
as he continues to make music
with his every spank.

He's a talented musician
in that he can play two
instruments at once.
The drummer's lover
in his lap moans and whimpers
as his flesh is slapped.
He provides the melody
to the rhythmic section
pounded out by
the drummer boy

Micky Omega

Stocking Stuffers

He works hard on his feet all day
so we can afford presents for the family.
He collapses on the bed with a sigh
and a hand reaching for pain relievers.

I am by no means a trad-boy-wife,
but on days like these, I like to kneel
and undo the laces of his leather shoes
and pull them away to reveal his pink socks.

His feet are warm between my kneading fingers,
expanding in their stockings like proving bread
so of course I place the fabric on my face
and breathe in the scent of gentle baking.

If it were up to me, I'd hang his socks
on the mantle to fill with little gifts,
perhaps like crusted loads of cum and kisses,
but he doesn't want the room to smell like feet.

Have you ever sat with someone's soles
pressed against the sides of your face
warming you from the winter cold outside
the door and sending heat to your loins?

He watches me peels his socks off
one by one and fold them against the floor,
fingers lingering on the soft, damp, and musky
cloth that signals all his love for me.

Christmas is Coming

My tongue rolls up his meaty stocking stuffers
and we sigh as one. We fish out our cocks
from our pants and massage them
much the way I worked his feet earlier.

A schoolboy's laugh spills from his lips
between moans when he grips my nose
between his big toe and whatever you call
the second one no one pays much attention to.

As my man moves my head in tiny circles,
I move his other foot down to my crotch.
Despite all his hard work, his skin is soft
as though it were made to be loved.

My tongue replaces my nose when he releases it,
and his head drops back on the mattress.
His tired hand begins to slow. He might ask me
to replace it, and I gladly would.

Until then, though, I stay at my lover's feet
and wash his skin with my saliva and pre-cum
as though I am Jesus, and this is the one
true act of salvation this Christmas season.

Micky Omega

Immaculate Conception

Y'know, Mary got pregnant despite being a virgin,
so God could be in our bedroom tonight, laughing
when you try to be all dom and serious and call me
a bitch, and He could choose to start another miracle,
to bless our holy union, to let you finally get me pregnant
and have the next savior be the son of two dorky gay guys
who are such complete and utter sluts for each other.

So fuck me, baby. Fuck me like the world depends on it.
Fuck me like our moans will save every sinner's soul.
Fuck me like I'm Mary and you're the Holy Ghost.
Fuck me like Christmas is coming.
Fuck me like only you can.

Snowflake

They say each crystalline drop
is unique in the cosmos
which sounds mathematically impossible
but what do I know,
I'm just a silly slut

So let me make a joke
about the melt-in-your-mouth goodness
of falling white cream
splashing on my extended tongue
and raining down my throat

Micky Omega

Three Wise Men

gather to write the long awaited sequel
to the Kama Sutra, this time detailing
all the positions three men can get
themselves in for sex and love.

You have the triangles, of course,
where each have a cock
in their mouths or a hole
on their tongue.

There's the Eiffel Tower in Paris
where one wise man is on all fours
while the other two fill his holes
and hold hands to add some romance.

At the insistence of St. Nick, they added
the Skier where one stands in front
and reaches back with his fists
to jerk off his ski poles on the mountain.

The Corn on the Cob is where two
are on their knees, moving their
gluttonous lips over the straining shaft
that glides between their kisses.

The Double Dog sends one of the kneeling
men up to join the saliva-lubed one
whilst the other stays in his happy place
with leaky dicks filling his mouth.

Christmas is Coming

Everyone already knows about the double-stuff
penetrations with a proper stretched out bottom
who can take plenty of wisdom inside him
but they take time to paint each way to do it.

You can lay with one man on his back,
one impaled lying on his chest,
and the third standing at attention
guiding the pounding pace.

You can have the two tops lay like scissor
sisters, get them kissing each others feet,
cocks held together with a cock ring
while the bottom rides them like a pogostick.

A fuck blow sandwich is made with bottom meat
between two pieces of consuming bread
where one fucks him hard and the other
draws out his mayonnaise with a mouth.

The Double Decker Pecker Bus
finds two bottoms clinging to each other
with their holes wet and ready
to be filled by their lover.

Everyone's favorite public transportation
is the train where a top gets a hole,
a bottom gets a cock, and a vers whore
gets the best of both worlds.

The Three Wise Men missed the Star
of Bethlehem shining bright because
they were too busy thinking up ways
to fuck each other like God would want.

Chestnuts

The pounding lust in my sternum
might be an inferno, an open fire
roasting the loose nuts that hang
from handsome, glistening sex
and bounce between my pecs,
tapping sticky skin against skin.

Women like to joke about how ugly
they find the folding skin of testicles
and I think that's the most confounding
difference between the sexes – not a
thing on the planet is more beautiful
than your hanging balls filled with need.

Your dancing fingers twist around
your tower cock and your halo hole
spasms around my own swirling digits.

Soon your roasting chestnuts will send
your seeds busting out over my face,
and we'll both lick away your delicacy.

My eyes flick between your nuts and eyes.

This is what it is to live bewitched by beauty.

Nutcracker

My thighs tense each time
he draws back his fingers.
He's going to tap again
like checking the bounce
of a jiggle cake.

Good boy, he says,
waiting for me to thank him
for the slight pain that comes
with every hiss I give.

He rises from the floor and
onto the bed, replacing his fingers
with his foot pressed on my sack.

He steps on me then gently kicks.
I cling to his other leg and moan.

I love how he loves this.

Micky Omega

Candy Cane II

There's a new challenge for horny gays
on their social media of choice:
You take a candy cane with a large hook,
hang it as an ornament on a tree you own,
and see how much of a candy store
you could stock with the length of your cock.

To put it in other words: your erection
is already a delicate dessert. Cover it
in sweets and be the proud owner of
a true candy cane.

Grinch

That hairy bastard has a heart
three times too small for his chest.
That's why his fingertips are cold
and he's always burying his frigid
toes into your thighs to warm them up.

Those little chills are smoke signals
sent to Whoville begging for connection,
for love, for help, for a flame to warm
his needy, frigid flesh. He's so hairy
to help keep him warm, didn't you know?

He's just a grumpy furry who has trouble
getting out of his fursona character.
In the run-up to Christmas, he steals
the gifts from your throbbing Christmas tree
in the hope you'll help take off his fursuit.

When the wolf comes out of his costume,
sweaty hair matted and damp skin shivering,
you'll find his heart is ever-expanding
like a cartoon character spotting a handsome
figure – that's you, you pretty beast.

Take his frozen digits and warm them
against your tongue. His heart won't be
the only thing to grow, but it will grow.
The Grinch will save Christmas with
grand romance and a fuzzy cuddle.

Micky Omega

Wrapping Paper

Look, everyone likes the pretty colors
of wrapping paper over presents,
the feel under the fingers when its torn,
and the sound of ripping.

It's safer to keep presents in their packages
and paper, sure, but doesn't everyone
want to get to the point where there's no
need for any of the decoration?

So, like, if we drop any pretentious metaphor,
this is all to say, I want you to cum inside me.
I don't want to toss your load in the trash
and taste rubber against your cock as I clean it.

Thrust all the way inside me, corkscrewing
your eyebrows and earthquaking your lips
as your spew into the deepest parts of me
as if we might be the boys to make life.

I want to feel your essence dribble
out of me and down my cheeks,
over my thighs, drying on my skin
through the days and nights.

It's apparently irresponsible to write
or film or celebrate unwrapped sex,
cocks bare of paper, but baby,
I am greedy. I want your everything.

Poinsettia

Do you know why they normally call
an asshole a rosebud, darling?

That gorgeous button blush of pink
is a source of stereotypical romance.

We're told to stop and smell the roses,
and everyone wants to sniff a clean hole.

If you hand a man a rose for no reason,
he'll get all cute and flustered.

If you offer a man your hole, he'll similarly
lose his mind to desire and joy.

Flowers are often found in gardens which works
as imagery since you don't shave.

Rose is a flavor in certain bakery goods
that can sometimes taste a bit like soap.

If you grab a rose wrong or a rosebud right,
you'll probably get struck with a prick.

But, my love, it is the holiday season, so we need
a more festive red flower to call your hole.

Your poinsettia is the reason for the season.
It's the holy beauty in the church.

Micky Omega

It's the flower I could kiss and care for
until its last petal settles into the earth.

I'm going to sprinkle snow onto your pretty
flower and then lick it clean once more.

You're so beautiful, baby. All I want for Christmas
is you, your heart, and your perfect poinsettia.

Cranberry Sauce

really is best when coming out of a can,
right? Like, we can all be agreed on that.
No one wants pulpy cranberry sauce
except for ancient people who mostly
like how they can use chunky juice
to make the rest of us uncomfortable.

Two lovers sat on a series of towels
on their bed with a thing of cranberry
sauce on a plate between them.
They two men grab fistfulls of sticky
gelatin and smack the globs against
the other's bare and giggling breasts.

It's a bit gross. They both think it's a bit
gross. But they keep going with unending
laughs between them as they slather
each other up like cornbread and dinner rolls
waiting to be piled up with turkey
and stuffing and some shaved phallic vegetable.

It's not long before their fingers zoom around
the plate trying to scoop out that last bit
of sauce. It winds up flying off the plate
and landing on one lover's thigh.
The other man bends down and licks
the tart sweet up with a curious tongue.

Micky Omega

Soon they rolled around on top the towels,
bed creaking likely out of second-hand
embarrassment as they lapped
at the sticky skin of their lover.
It clung to their skin and hair and tongue.
They were half tempted to go straight to a bath.

It wasn't often the two tried something new,
and for it to be so delightfully weird and awkward
and sort of unenjoyable was, paradoxically,
quite nice. To try a new sex thing with your lover
and discover that you hate it in a funny way
is the sort of sticky holiday gift most can only dream of.

Years from now, they would joke about cranberries
spread on their titties and guts and cocks.
They'd laugh at the most random of times
at the memory. One would come home with a can
and the other would lose his goddamn mind,
crying through the raucous laughter.

Who knows? Maybe if they didn't try
a weird sex thing people would judge them for,
they might have broken up and lost
out on love. They would have turned their backs
on each other and on trying new weird sex things.
God truly blessed the cranberries.

Parade

The Folsom Street Christmas Pride Parade
sees plenty of men suffering for beauty
if you define beauty to be sluttiness,
which happens to be my definition.

Twinkle lights line the leather straps
of their harnesses and ornaments hang
from the tips of their fuzzy butt plug tails
that help keep them at least a bit warm.

Happy pups with Santa hats march as a pack
down the road, slowly losing members
as they peel off to play fetch with Yule
logs lugged around by the daddies and bears.

A marching band plays R&B arrangements
of Christmas songs, banging on their drums
as the onlookers bang away at each other
to summon forth a happy holiday.

It's a white Christmas at the parade
with the gay otters swimming down
the rivers of flooding cum that have turned
Folsom into a sexy Venice.

Micky Omega

Ghost of Christmas Past

Nothing quite puts one in the holiday spirit
like watching old homemade videos on VHS
but no one uses those anymore so
we'll have to settle for digital films
stored on the cloud.

Speaking of clouds, might as well light up
to watch these flicks, kiss me and breathe
smoke into my lungs, and kick back
with a giggle while we watch
our old bodies fucking.

In our first year together, we dressed
as elves tasked with making and testing
sex toys, so we spent hours with silicone
on our lips, nips, and dicks, plunging
them inside each other's caverns.

Who could forget the year we covered
you in pretty pink bows under the tree?
I added some film grain in editing
to really give it that old time feel,
make our amateur porn something artistic.

We've made more Christmas films together
than any Christian movie production company
out there on the planet. It takes effort to come
up with new plots and shots, but we'll figure
it out, my darling Star of Bethlehem.

Christmas is Coming

You know, the Library of Congress
would probably be interested
in these works of art
celebrating the
American man.

We'll get back to filming next week. Yes,
I invited the twink, the bear, and the wolf,
oh my! We'll ravish them and they'll ravish us.
I'll edit them so on Christmas day, we can sit
on the couch and watch.

Church

Let's sneak out of the Nativity play
and the unending sermon neither
of us care much about and head
to your sedan waiting out in the dark
parking lot, in the cold with its tinted
windows, and let's do something
really holy. I have a halo to offer you,
if you catch my drift. We'll be crying
out *God* and *Hallelujah* at the same
time as the congregation. They'll rise
to their feet while ours are busy shaking,
toes curling, shivering in the chill
and pleasure. They'll take communion
while we're busy with communion.
I'll speak in tongues as the car shakes.
You can get on your knees on the
floorboards and pray with an open mouth.

Icicle

You have to be careful
when making an icicle.

You don't want the cold
to hurt your partner's cock.

Pay attention to how they kiss
and moan and squirm.

Melt the ice cube a bit
with your tongue and lips.

Get him leaking in swirling torrents
of melting cold and heated saliva.

Like all icicles, it will eventually fall
until you mold it back up again.

Get your tongue stuck to that frigid
flesh like a telephone pole in the cold.

Melt it in your mouth
then keep it there.

Drink, baby,
drink.

Micky Omega

Up on the Housetop

underneath the glittering stars,
there's a wool blanket waiting
for our bare backs to grace it.

Maybe if the angels we have heard
while high see us in the warm
Southern nights of Texas, they'll take
the challenge and send us snow.

They way I'm going to kiss you
with one hand on the back of your head
and the other cupped inside your pants
will make St. Gabriel blow his horn.

Angels will flood the skies and flurry down
so they too might make love with men
and feel a cock hardening in their grasp
while a handsome someone moans in their mouth.

I think the heavens will be disappointed
to discover that no man on the planet
holds a single scented candle to you,
my beautiful, sexy man.

They'll flock to our rooftop and demand
we make love in front of them so they might
learn what it is they've been found longing
in their season of fucking men.

Christmas is Coming

When they beg for our secret, for a love-making
guide that creates our sort of sex,
all I'll do for them if cry out your name
over and over until they get the hint.

It's you. You are Eros, Aphrodite, Christmas,
Valentines, and everything else. If you grew
a tail tomorrow, I'd cum while kissing it.
I'll make love to whatever you become.

Jingle Bells

Batman smells, as the young people say.
It's an accurate little parody song this year,
at least if you consider that Christmas
starts as soon as Halloween ends,
and this year, you dressed up
as the Caped Crusader.

When you peel off your costume after
the parties at the bars, you do smell.
You've been dancing all night, after all,
sweating in the heavy fabric and plastic
and soaking your skin and hair
in that pheromone musk of yours.

Flex for me, I request after you put the mask
back on. When you do, I bend my nose
into the bat cave of your pit
and take a deep whiff.
My head buzzes, my eyes roll back,
and I start to moan and whimper.

After such a long day spent saving the city
out in the cold, a hero deserve to relax,
to be worshiped. We both know this,
so you press my face into your damp skin
and command me to lick. You need a bath,
and I need to serve, so make use of my tongue.

Christmas is Coming

It isn't long before you're pushing me down
to my knees in our bedroom. *If you think that's good,
get a load of these bad boys.* You jiggle your balls.
Heat spills off them. They hang lower
than your cock which soon grows against my face
as I take in the smell and taste of your jingle bells.

Jack Frost

People say the winters haven't been as cold
because of global warming, and they're right,
of course, but that isn't the full story.

Mother Nature's eldest son, that ice twink
Jack Frost has recently become a circuit
gay, a party bottom at the clubs.

He's a chubby chaser, really, hanging around
gatherings of bears and trying to get lost
in bear hugs and sandwiches.

He loves the warmth of hair and the feeling
of weight against his back, of a stomach
against his ice-pole cock.

Jack can't grow anything on account
of his blue thumbs, but he loves to provide.
He'll feed you until you're about to burst.

His mother has to call him up and rouse him
from his slumber packed between two husbears
to remind him he has a duty to bring the cold.

Jack Frost blows through towns in a hurry.
When he lingers, it's because he's busy
feeding and eating a thicc (with five Cs) ass.

Christmas is Coming

Fret not. While he's in his chasing state,
he'll come to hate the heat. After all,
people shave when it's hot out.

Eventually, he'll cycle back around to being Father
Christmas, fucking twinks with collars on
and sending Noels filled with white.

Jack Frost is a jack of all trades,
meaning he's a verse switch,
ever changing, fucking every type he can.

Micky Omega

Gingerbread Man

Is there anything better
than being a gingerbread man
ready to be eaten with icing
leaking out your freshly
fucked and ginger bred hole?

No one on the planet
is better at sticking their tongue
in your ass than a man
with a red mustache on his lip
who just spent thirty minutes supplying his load.

Eat me, sir. Tell me how sweet
you taste spilling out of me.
Tell me how you wish
I could be your every meal
and take your every load.

Gingerbread House

You know what they say: friends who
cum together, come together forever.
There's also the more modern saying:
friends who build gingerbread houses
together in a competitive way, naked
in one of their kitchen end up closer
and happier than any other friends.

It's such a common saying that I'm sure
everyone you know spends a day
each year fucking and sucking and sticking
together slabs of gingerbread.

Gay groups have it best, though.
We get to bring a supply of semen
to spill and mix in the icing.
We built this city out of cookies and cum.
Really, isn't that how you build
any community? When I eat
my gingerbread house, I'll take
the lifeblood blossoming seeds
of the men I trust my life with.
Their loads linger as an aftertaste
from the sweet icing and fragrant cookies.

When I have a rough day, I get on my knees
and my friends turn me into a gingerbread
man, put back together with their cum
holding the cracks.

Gifts for Pets

Time for celebration
Time for gifts
Gifts for thanks
Gifts for good boys
Boys in pup hoods
Boys worshiping cock
Cock delicious
Cock for kissing
Kiss his nose
Kiss his hole
Hole for filling
Hole for bones
Bones are gifts
Bones need licks
Licks on your feet
Licks on your pits
Pits ripe with scent
Pits cleaned with tongue
Tongue his ass
Tongue his sack
Sacks for squeezing
Sacks for tea
Teabag him in the morning
Tea while he sucks
Sucks your cock
Sucks your soul
Soul-saving kisses
Soul-shaking orgasms
Orgasmic love
Orgasm from only anal
Anal fisting
Anal felching

Christmas is Coming

Felching out snow
Felching your cum
Cum inside him
Cum on his face
Face the future
Face each other
Others disappear
Other become self
Selfies with him sucking
Self-denial in his cage
Cage for sleep
Cage of love
Love yous spoken
Love through pets
Pets for fucking
Pets for your love
Love
Fucking

Micky Omega

Candy Cane III

Hey handsome,
I've got this sweet tooth
I just can't satisfy
with chocolate or sugar.

Howdy hot stuff,
the doctors diagnosed me
with a terminal case of
an oral fixation.

'Sup sexy,
I remember you've got candy
tucked away in the magic
of your boulder bulge.

Greetings gay,
your candy cane
is the sweetest thing
I've ever tasted.

Salutations sugar,
all of this to say, if you want,
I could spend so long sucking
you, you forget I'm not your cock.

I'll press my tongue to your frenulum
and your taint, swirling circles
summoning forth those sweet
little moans you promised me.

Call me by your name this holiday,
because baby, I'm yours to use,

Christmas is Coming

body and soul, bound to the music
of the squelch of your cock.

These craving pangs in my gut
can only be comforted away
by indulging my sweet tooth
on your flesh and your cum.

I've been ever so hungry since
I first laid eyes on you, and somehow
every kiss and every date since
have only deepened my gluttony.

I could feast on actual food
until they made some exploitative
documentary about my pain,
and still I'd be starved without you.

When I plod to the kitchen
for a midnight snack, really
I want to shake you awake
and steal every kiss you have left.

When I wake and cook breakfast,
I'd rather have breakfast in bed:
sausage, eggs, a donut hole,
and cream. I want you.

Baby, it's the holidays,
so this time of year,
call it a candy cane
and satisfy my hunger.

Micky Omega

Hot Chocolate

Rush in from the cold, building snowmen
like we were once again giggling children,
noses red and cheeks flushed as though
tomorrow we'll be sick as payment for
today's fun. Turn on the electric fireplace,
crackling beneath the mantle television
where Hallmark movies play silly mushy
stuff that used to only be for the straights.
I'll make us hot chocolate with many mini
Marshmallows, sticky swirling white sending
my mind straight into the gutter like tomorrow's
melting snow. The warm mugs in our hands
are exorcists for the ghosts of the cold.

We'll sip together under a thick duvet
with nothing else on our skin but each other,
limbs tangled up as we thaw and shiver
and become human once more.
You'll look over with that smirk that always
gets you whatever you want. *I know
a better way to warm up*, you'll say.
We'll burrow under the heavy cover
with hot breath and wandering fingers.
Our dancing tongues will taste like hot chocolate.

Christmas is Coming

It's a toss-up whose legs will wrap around
whose back, curling toes when cock fills
needy hole, bathed in the warmth
of a handsome man's depths.
We'll rock and fuck until we overheat
and toss the duvet to the floor. We'll breathe
in a heap on the couch and lay watching movies
until the night sets into cuddling sleep
and we wake in the morning with marshmallow
to spill into each other's mouths.

Micky Omega

Chocolate Kisses

Have you ever noticed that those dollops
of chocolate pressed into brown sugar
cookies look a lot like thick pert nipples
standing at jolly attention against round
areolas, begging for a mouth to suck
on them, for teeth to gently scrape their surface?

I get horny in a bakery thinking of pressing
the kisses to my lips like pushing you
to the mattress, lifting your shirt, and
swirling my tongue around your sensitive
nipples surrounded by their forest of hair
or, better, extra sensitive just after a shave.

Giftbox

Listen, babe, I know it's juvenile,
but the first gift I got you for Christmas…
It's my dick in a box!

See, I knew you'd laugh. Oh shit, babe,
are you crying? Was it a bad…? Oh,
it's just so stupid and funny. Thank god.

I got one of those kits that let you
make a dildo out of your own cock
and balls – It's important to have a flared base!

See, this way, when I'm out for work
or you're off visiting friends across
the country, I can still fuck you.

I know you love the feel of that big dorsal
vein against the tip of your tongue
and the ridge of my head on your hole.

Of course you can use it on your friends
and your fans and your collaborators.
Baby, what's mine is yours.

Now I can fuck you at both ends
whenever you want, just like you dreamed
about and texted me during dinner.

Micky Omega

Should you make an onahole based on
your hole? Well I'm sure it'd sell pretty well.
We'd make a decent chunk of change.

I'd kiss it and fuck it every night when
I'm away, of course, but I'd almost prefer
to save all my loads for you when I return.

Merry Christmas, baby.
I love you to the moon and back.
Of course you can sit on it now.

Snowball

There's something so beautiful about a snowball,
something nearly divine in the packed falling white.

Hephaestus would take the dazzling pearls and attempt
to forge them into a necklace beautiful enough for his wife.

I stick my tongue out for the snow, to catch and savor
the holy rain that drips from your battered pink hole.

There is much I have done with my life: projects,
successes, and friendships I am proper proud of.

Yet my grandest act of beauty will forever be loading
you up with slippery white to snowball fall on my lips.

Micky Omega

Ghost of Christmas Present

Real men wear make-up.
Specifically, concealer.
Specifically, to cover up bruises.
Specifically, the bruises left by your lips.
Specifically, when they sucked and pulled at my neck.
Specifically, on the left side of my Adam's apple.
Specifically, from that time on Christmas.
Specifically, the fifth time we fucked that day.
Specifically, when we were frotting.
Specifically, when I was whimpering.
Specifically, when my legs were in the air.
Specifically, right as I was begging you.
Specifically, begging you to fuck me.
Specifically, asking for daddy's cock.
Specifically, your fat hairy dick.
Specifically, for it to breed me.
Specifically, to make a mess with the loads already there.
Specifically, the ones you shot in before dinner.
Specifically, the dinner with your family.
Specifically, the one where I wore a bandana.
Specifically, to cover the other hickeys.
Specifically, the ones on the back of my neck.
Specifically, from when you bit me.
Specifically, when you took me from behind.
Specifically, right when I woke in your arms and cried.
Specifically, cried how much I love you.
Specifically, more than Achilles loved Patroclus.

Christmas is Coming

Specifically, deeper than the Marianas Trench.
Specifically, I want my legacy to be yours.
Specifically, I want my name to meld with yours.
Specifically, I want to be known for our merging.
Specifically, the way our hearts twist together.
Specifically, the way our bodies melt into each other.
Specifically, the way I cling to you when we make love.

Those are the exact hickeys I'm wearing make-up to hide.
The rest of them? Well, that's why I'm wearing clothes.

Micky Omega

Pinetree

They sell little bundles of sticks
that smell like forests, so sort of
like you when you dab cologne.

If we buy a few, none of our friends
will smell the amount of sex
we have all over the place.

We can place them like mistletoe
over every door frame to blast
their noses with the scent of Christmas trees.

When we throw them all out,
we'll no longer be nose blind to brilliant scent
of the ways we've loved each other in every room.

Naughty List

Do you know what happens to naughty boys?

They get bent over Santa's lap
and find why he's the master
toymaker as he makes you his toy.

They sputter and spill snot and throat slime
all over his candy cane while he holds
their head down on his sweets.

They get a thick neoprene collar and
a leash stuck on their neck while
they're trained on how to be good.

They cocks locked up as little nubs
in chastity cages that prevent them
from cumming until Santa allows them.

They find fingers tapping against their cheeks,
their useless sacks, their cages,
and their whimpering holes.

They stretch with the cuffs on their ankles
and wrists binding them to the corners
of the cool winter bed.

Micky Omega

They tremble from the feathers on their feet,
brushing over their taint, swirling over
their straining nipples.

Bad boys get fucked for hours.
Their holes get battered by all of Santa's
workshop with its dozens of elves.

So my question to you, my sweet little bitch boy,
is what list you're hoping I'll write you down on:
naughty or nice?

Nice List

Baby, after everything you've done for me,
the way you call me name, the little texts
you send asking how I'm doing, the way
you curl into me when we're on the couch,
how you watch each and every dumbass
TikTok and YouTube video I message you,
how you let me sit between your legs after
a rough day and play with my hair to relax me,
how your eyes always beg for a kiss with
you legs wrapped around me, how you moan
my name into my mouth while you beg for me
to fill you up with my cum and manage a miracle
by getting my precious boy pregnant, the videos
you send with my briefs pressed desperate
against your nose while you massage your cock,
after all of that, of course you're on my nice list.
You're a good boy. You're my good boy.
You're my everything that I could ever want.
So I want you to step into the shower
and get ready for every reward I can think
to gift you with tonight.

Micky Omega

Partridge

Apparently you won't actually find
any partridges in pear trees –
They're ground birds who don't
like getting high, the sober kings.

Christmas is magic, as they say,
which is why that first day's gift
is something rare that maybe
shouldn't be, something only for you.

I suppose we're both little birds
in that you aren't often found atop trees
and I'm not normally the one buried
amongst pears, yet here we are.

It's a gift to step outside of normalcy,
to trust and love someone enough
to offer up that part of you so rare
you might call its presence a miracle.

Sing me your birdsong carol
as I slip inside your warm fruit
with kisses on your neck
and whispered cries of love.

Scrooge

Grumpy men who can't stand the holidays
are filled with such wonderful resentment
they need to get out somehow, so if you
bed one in December, goddamn, your
eyes will roll into the back of your head
and you'll start hallucinating from the stabs
of pleasure blasting up your spine from
the hole they make sure to properly own.
If you're not wanting the whole romance
thing during Christmas, if you just want
the life and the worries and winter blues
fucked right out of you, your best bet
is to find a grumpy guy complaining
about how he doesn't like such grand,
ostentatious displays of opulence and joy,
and turn that Scrooge into a Screwge.

12 Days

On the first day of Christmas
my true love gave to me
a facial in the morning.

On the second day of Christmas
my true love gave to me
two onaholes,
and a facial in the morning.

On the third day of Christmas
my true love gave to me
three rimmings,
two onaholes,
and a facial in the morning.

On the fourth day of Christmas
my true love gave to me
four vibrators,
three rimmings, two onaholes,
and a facial in the morning.

On the fifth day of Christmas
my true love gave to me
five orgasms,
four vibrators,
three rimmings, two onaholes,
and a facial in the morning.

Christmas is Coming

On the sixth day of Christmas
my true love gave to me
six Frenching kisses,
five orgasms, four vibrators,
three rimmings, two onaholes,
and a facial in the morning.

On the seventh day of Christmas
my true love gave to me
seven inches in me,
six Frenching kisses,
five orgasms, four vibrators,
three rimmings, two onaholes,
and a facial in the morning.

On the eighth day of Christmas
my true love gave to me
eight friends to fuck me,
seven inches in me, six Frenching kisses,
five orgasms, four vibrators,
three rimmings, two onaholes,
and a facial in the morning.

On the ninth day of Christmas
my true love gave to me
nine nipple twisties,
eight friends to fuck me,
seven inches in me, six Frenching kisses,
five orgasms, four vibrators,
three rimmings, two onaholes,
and a facial in the morning.

Micky Omega

On the tenth day of Christmas
my true love gave to me
ten tickling fingers
nine nipple twisties,
eight friends to fuck me,
seven inches in me, six Frenching kisses,
five orgasms, four vibrators,
three rimmings, two onaholes,
and a facial in the morning.

On the eleventh day of Christmas
my true love gave to me
eleven spanks on my ass,
ten tickling fingers
nine nipple twisties,
eight friends to fuck me,
seven inches in me, six Frenching kisses,
five orgasms, four vibrators,
three rimmings, two onaholes,
and a facial in the morning.

On the twelfth day of Christmas
my true love gave to me
twelve friends to fuck me,
eleven spanks on my ass,
ten tickling fingers
nine nipple twisties,
eight friends to fuck me,
seven inches in me, six Frenching kisses,
five orgasms, four vibrators,
three rimmings, two onaholes,
and a facial in the morning.

Ghost of Christmas Future

With this leather cockring in a fancy
box filled with velvet almost as pretty
and soft as the flesh in your hole,
I do humbly ask to spend every
Christmas with you hereon.

And on each Christmas morning,
I'll kneel as I do now in front of you
to thread your manhood through this ring
and into my waiting, eager mouth.

We'll video call our families with your cum
still linger on my tongue with its
sweet and salty tang.

I'll tell you how the best gift I could ask for
is to spend another day with you.

Haunt and fuck me every year, my dear.

Micky Omega

Shepherd

Stand tall with a strong grip
on your towering staff
and all the fluffy herd,
the entire pack of pup boys
will go where you lead them,
race down the streets to the club,
pile in the apartment with shy blushes,
jump into a pile of moaning bodies.

Handlers are important in the community.
They know how to spot pups who haven't
discovered their need to don a hood yet,
and they know how to coax men into a space
where they can bark and frolic and play.
It's so hard to learn how to play again
once you're grown, isn't it?

It feels selfish to be happy,
but it isn't. It's true. It's right.
Shepherds know how to remind you
of your duty to be happy. They'll give you
head pets and plug your hole with a tail.
They'll give you a bone to slobber on
whenever you're a good boy.

Praise be to the handlers,
to those who know how to summon
happiness and pleasure.
Praise be to their pets.
Praise be to the shepherds.
Praise be to their sheep.
Praise kinks are the best.

Manger

The manger is a holy place,
isolated for the birth of a savior
out in a barn in Bethlehem.

So really, fucking out here
is nothing short of heaven-blessed
and perfect for the season.

You fuck where you can get to
which is to say you fuck wherever
you think you can get away with it.

White Christmas

In an ideal world,
you'd cream in my coffee.
You'd provide icing for my breakfast.
You'd cum on my face. You'd fill my mouth.
You'd splatter semen all over my shaking back.
You'd unload in my ass and use it as lube to keep going
and cream inside me time after time.

I fantasize about a world where sex is natural,
where I can lean over on the subway and give you head,
where you can pull me into the bathroom and fuck in the stall,
where I can jerk you off at the bar as we drink,
where everyone can see how good of a boy I can be for you,
where we go to the movie theater and I can sit in your lap,
where I don't have to hide my whimpers at your touch,
where I can look at your face and get hard like at home,
where I can kiss you on every street, in every store,
where I can walk around with your cum on my lips
like a claiming mark declaring that we are each other's

Every holiday should be a white holiday
and by that I mean it should be a celebration
of you and I, with every inch of our bodies coated,
soaking, dripping, glistening with beautiful cum.

Christmas is Coming

About the Author

Micky Omega is a gay adult performer and erotica author who wants to celebrate and explore every corner of desire, no matter the weird corners to which it might extend. This good boy loves submission, poetry, and music.

* 9 7 9 8 2 2 7 0 5 5 5 4 5 *